EXPLORING
CAREERS

D0001996

Careers in Education

Barbara Sheen

ReferencePoint
Press®

About the Author

Barbara Sheen is the author of eighty-seven books for young people. She lives in New Mexico with her family. In her spare time she likes to swim, garden, cook, and walk. She is a retired teacher.

© 2016 ReferencePoint Press, Inc.
Printed in the United States

For more information, contact:
ReferencePoint Press, Inc.
PO Box 27779
San Diego, CA 92198
www.ReferencePointPress.com

Picture Credits:
Maury Aaseng: 6
Thinkstock Images: 26, 47, 51

LIBRARY OF CONGRESS CATALOGING-IN-PUBLICATION DATA

Sheen, Barbara.
  Careers in education : by Barbara Sheen.
    pages cm. -- (Exploring careers)
  Includes bibliographical references and index.
    ISBN 978-1-60152-808-7 (hardback) -- ISBN 1-60152-808-6 (hardback) 1. Education--Vocational guidance--United States--Juvenile literature. 2. Teaching--Vocational guidance--United States--Juvenile literature. I. Title.
  LB1775.2.S48   2015
  371.4'25--dc23

                                                                    2014040440

Contents

Introduction: Making a Difference   4

College Professor   9

Curriculum Developer   17

Early Childhood Educator   25

Education Administrator   34

K–12 Teacher   42

Library Media Specialist   50

School Counselor   58

Special Education Teacher   66

Interview with a Special Education Teacher   74

Other Careers in Education   77

Index   78

Making a Difference

Education is an integral part of American life. Approximately 50.1 million students attend American elementary and secondary schools. About 21.8 million more attend degree-granting colleges and universities. These numbers do not include the millions of young children who attend preschools and day care facilities. Nor does it take into account the individuals who attend vocational training institutes to learn specific trades that help them gain employment. Workers in almost all careers receive in-house training to improve their job skills. Even when education is not required to gain or retain employment, many people take classes in diverse subjects to enhance their personal growth. Indeed, lifelong learning is an important part of twenty-first-century life.

All of these learners depend on educators. The American education system is one of the nation's largest employers. As of 2014 approximately 3.7 million full-time teachers were employed in American elementary and secondary schools alone. But teachers are not the only professionals employed in the education industry. Educators also serve as school counselors, administrators, teacher's aides, and library media specialists. They are coaches, early childhood educators, curriculum specialists, and employee training specialists. School social workers, educational diagnosticians, and speech-language pathologists are also part of the education industry. So are school psychologists, school nurses, and postsecondary instructors. Other professionals like registrars, school bus drivers, attendance clerks, school secretaries, custodians, and cafeteria managers are essential to keeping schools running smoothly. In addition, textbook authors and editors, educational software developers, and instructional designers are responsible for preparing materials that help students learn.

A Versatile Profession

Individuals who want a career in education have many choices. They can choose to work in a teaching or nonteaching position in a variety of educational environments. They also can choose to work with infants, children, teens, or adults. Those who teach can specialize in a particular subject area. For instance, most elementary teachers work with students ranging from five to eleven years old. They teach a mixture of academic subjects as well as help students develop learning skills. Middle school, high school, and college instructors focus on a specific subject. This allows individuals who are passionate about a particular field of study such as math, technology, art, or science to share their knowledge and enthusiasm with others.

Some educators specialize in working with students with distinctive needs. English as a second language (ESL or ESOL) instructors, for example, help adults or children whose primary language is not English become proficient in English. They also help students acculturate to American life through activities like field trips and holiday celebrations.

Other important education professions suit individuals who might not be interested in providing daily classroom instruction. School nurses, for example, support students' academic success by monitoring and ministering to their physical health. They provide first aid to sick or injured students, and through annual screenings, they identify health issues that impact student achievement. In fact, these professionals are often the first to detect that a student needs eyeglasses or a hearing aid. And if a student needs help in getting these, a school social worker connects them to an appropriate social agency. Educators can work in diverse environments. These include public and private schools, college and universities, and community agencies. Educators are also found in businesses, museums and cultural centers, and government-sponsored programs. They work in hospitals and in the military. They are employed in all fifty states, and many work abroad for the US Department of Defense, private schools, and organizations like the Peace Corps. Finally, some

Position Comparisons

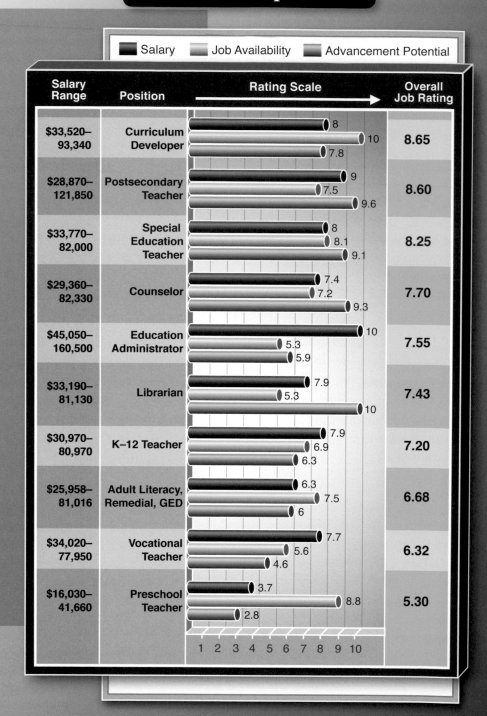

Legend: Salary · Job Availability · Advancement Potential

Salary Range	Position	Rating Scale	Overall Job Rating
$33,520–93,340	Curriculum Developer	Salary 8 · Job Availability 10 · Advancement Potential 7.8	8.65
$28,870–121,850	Postsecondary Teacher	Salary 9 · Job Availability 7.5 · Advancement Potential 9.6	8.60
$33,770–82,000	Special Education Teacher	Salary 8 · Job Availability 8.1 · Advancement Potential 9.1	8.25
$29,360–82,330	Counselor	Salary 7.4 · Job Availability 7.2 · Advancement Potential 9.3	7.70
$45,050–160,500	Education Administrator	Salary 10 · Job Availability 5.3 · Advancement Potential 5.9	7.55
$33,190–81,130	Librarian	Salary 7.9 · Job Availability 5.3 · Advancement Potential 10	7.43
$30,970–80,970	K–12 Teacher	Salary 7.9 · Job Availability 6.9 · Advancement Potential 6.3	7.20
$25,958–81,016	Adult Literacy, Remedial, GED	Salary 6.3 · Job Availability 7.5 · Advancement Potential 6	6.68
$34,020–77,950	Vocational Teacher	Salary 7.7 · Job Availability 5.6 · Advancement Potential 4.6	6.32
$16,030–41,660	Preschool Teacher	Salary 3.7 · Job Availability 8.8 · Advancement Potential 2.8	5.30

Rating scale: 1 2 3 4 5 6 7 8 9 10

Source: Top Ten Reviews, "Education Careers Review," 2014. http://education-careers-review.toptenreviews.com.

educators are self-employed. They operate small businesses such as tutoring services, driving schools, preschools, day care centers, or dance or music studios, among other options.

Why Become an Educator?

Individuals become educators for a variety of reasons. In uncertain economic times, a career in education offers individuals a higher level of job security than other, more volatile fields. Generally, positions that are vacated as educators retire, advance to other positions, or leave the field must be filled by new hires. New positions are also created to service the nation's expanding population. The Bureau of Labor Statistics (BLS) reports that from 2012 to 2022, total employment in the United States is predicted to increase by about 10.8 percent. Careers in education, however, are predicted to increase by 11.1 percent. Moreover, shortages of teachers in certain fields such as special education, math, science, technology, ESOL, and bilingual education raise the demand for educators, as does the lack of instructors in specific geographic regions such as urban and rural schools in the southern and western parts of the United States. Additionally, most jobs in the field offer excellent benefits, including health insurance and retirement benefits. The work hours and the short school year, too, attract many people to the profession. Most educators enjoy long paid vacations, which include one to two months off in the summer, a paid winter and spring break, and a forty-hour workweek. This affords individuals time to study, travel, pursue a hobby, and spend time with their family.

The rewards of a career in education go beyond these practical factors. When asked, many educators say they entered the field in order to make a difference in the world. Educators do more than help students develop intellectually; they help students acquire the skills they need to prepare for successful lives. They serve as role models and mentors. For some students a teacher, principal, coach, adult education instructor, college professor, counselor, or teacher's aide may be the most memorable person in their lives. As Mary Rycik, chair of early childhood education at Ashland University in Ohio, explains on the university's website: "Teachers have the power to positively affect the lives of hundreds of people. Over the course of a 30 year career, with an average class of 25 per year, 750 children will learn to read, write, compute, reason, analyze, create, evaluate and prepare for their future lives thanks to you." There are very few professions that have such a far-reaching impact on so many lives.

College Professor

What Does a College Professor Do?

College professors are scholars who serve as teachers and researchers. Specializing in areas that range from academic subjects like history, mathematics, and literature to career-related fields like nursing, criminology, and law, they instruct college and university undergraduate and graduate students. In any given day these professionals may present a lecture to several hundred students, conduct a small graduate seminar, or supervise students' laboratory work. In addition to instructing students, they conduct original research in their field of study. In an article in the *Huffington Post*, University of Connecticut president Susan Herbst explains, "At research universities, like UConn, teaching undergraduate courses and graduate seminars are similar to one's 'day job,' in that it represents only part of what faculty must do. In addition to that, they must also conduct research, whether it's in a laboratory, a library or a site halfway across the world."

Professors publish the results of their research in journals and

At a Glance:
College Professor

Minimum Educational Requirements
Master's degree; many professorial positions require a doctorate

Personal Qualities
Good communication skills
Extensive expertise in a particular field of study

Certification and Licensing
None

Working Conditions
Indoors in colleges and universities

Salary Range
From $64,759 to $218,033

Number of Jobs
As of 2014 about 1,267,700

Future Job Outlook
Better than average

books. Many professors write or edit textbooks, too. Those involved in the arts are encouraged to practice their craft. University of Cincinnati English professor Michael Griffith says, "As faculty we get to do what we care about doing. I'm a fiction writer. UC gives me the opportunity to do my teaching and still write."

There are four types of full-time college professors: instructors, assistant professors, associate professors, and full professors. Full professors are the highest ranking of the group, followed by associate professors, assistant professors, and finally, instructors.

Professors may teach a number of classes per semester or only a few. Those employed by community colleges usually spend more time teaching than those in large research-oriented universities. In general, professors spend an average of ten to fifteen hours a week in actual instruction. This does not include the time they spend preparing for classes. Out-of-class work entails preparing lectures, a course syllabus, exams, and lesson plans; grading papers; and meeting with students to go over their progress during scheduled office hours. Plus, in order to keep up with new advances in their field, professors devote many hours to professional development.

The rest of their time is usually occupied by research and publication. Professors carry out research to add to their area of study, advance human knowledge, and help society. Research conducted by college professors has led to the discovery of cures for illnesses, the creation of new technology, a clearer understanding of historical figures and events, archaeological finds, and the development of methods to protect fragile ecosystems, among countless other contributions. Indeed, hundreds of college professors have won the Nobel Prize for their contributions to society.

Once professors complete a study, they write articles, papers, essays, and books based on the results. Traditionally, publishing a considerable amount of work is essential for lower-ranking college educators to advance to full professor. Therefore, most professors are under pressure to publish, and many publish a high volume of work in the course of their career. For instance, John Robert Greene, who has been a history and government professor at Cazenovia College in Syracuse, New York, for more than thirty years, has written or edited seventeen books on American history and politics, published more than one hundred articles and reviews, and served as a commentator and script advisor for a number of documentary programs.

How Do You Become a College Professor?

Education

To prepare for a career as a college professor, high school students should take courses that prepare them for college, as well as courses that focus on their field of interest. Becoming a college professor involves a considerable commitment to education. A master's degree is usually the minimum requirement for employment in community and junior colleges, with most colleges and universities requiring a doctorate or other terminal degree for the specific field of study. This path of progress entails four years of college-level study to earn a bachelor's degree, followed by one to two years to acquire a master's degree, and then another two to six years to obtain a doctoral degree. Depending on the university and the field of study, admissions to graduate programs can be highly competitive. Course work can be challenging. Classes focus on the student's particular field of study. In addition to successfully completing from thirty to forty hours of graduate-level course credits, master's degree candidates usually have to write a successful thesis and pass an oral exam in which they show a high level of competency in their subject area. Doctoral candidates are typically expected to successfully complete between forty-eight and seventy-two hours of graduate-level course credit, conduct research, write and defend a doctoral dissertation based on their research, and teach some undergraduate classes. It is not uncommon for prospective college professors to complete a postdoctoral fellowship. This involves an additional two to three years of research and publication upon completion of a doctoral degree.

Certification and Licensing

College professors are not required to have a special certificate or license. However, those in certain vocational fields such as nursing, engineering, law, medicine, and architecture, for example, usually are expected to hold a license in their field.

Volunteer Work and Internships

There are many ways individuals can prepare for a career as a professor. For undergraduates, working in a paid or voluntary position in the departmental office of one's major is a good way to learn more about the field. It also provides individuals with the opportunity to interact and network with professors who may serve as mentors or provide students with references for graduate school and future employment.

Another way to learn more is by helping a professor or graduate student with research. Such positions may be paid or volunteer. Taking part in a research project gives candidates a chance to observe the research process, work with a research group, and contribute to scholarly knowledge. Most colleges provide descriptions of research opportunities on departmental or school websites. Moreover, some universities have an office of undergraduate research that connects interested students with research projects. External research centers, too, often offer paid and unpaid positions to college students. Taking an independent study class that provides formal supervision and structure for undergraduates who want to do independent research is another way to experience the research process.

Doing an internship or taking a summer job related to one's chosen field of study, such as working in a museum for an art history major or at a newspaper for a journalism major, is another way to become more knowledgeable in a subject area. Most colleges help students find and arrange internships. Other possibilities include volunteering in schools or community centers or working in a summer camp. Such work gives individuals insight into what it is like to instruct others. Finally, accompanying a professor through a workday or sitting in on various levels of classes is another good way to learn about the profession.

Skills and Personality

College professors are scholars. A passion for learning is a key character trait of these professionals. This includes a love of reading, writing, studying, and researching to acquire a high level of expertise in a disciplinary field. Excellent communication skills are vital, too. Professors not only must know their field of study really well, they must be able to effectively convey knowledge to students and peers. Establishing a good rapport with students, faculty members, research assistants, college administrators, and editors is also essential. This requires good interpersonal skills. Other important personality traits include being persistent and a good problem solver. These characteristics can help professors achieve goals. Research projects, for example, do not always go well. To succeed, professors cannot be easily discouraged or frustrated, and they must be able to come up with solutions to whatever problems arise.

On the Job

Employers

Most professors are employed by private and public colleges and universities in undergraduate and graduate programs. These institutions include junior colleges, community colleges, four-year colleges, universities, and professional schools such as medical schools, law schools, and dental schools.

Working Conditions

Colleges and universities are typically clean, pleasant workplaces. Most professors have their own office or share an office with a colleague. College departments usually have secretaries and student workers that help professors with clerical tasks. Beyond scheduled classes and office hours, a professor's work schedule is usually flexible. Most work five days per week, nine months per year with a three-month summer break and a one- or two-week winter and spring break. Classes are generally held Monday through Friday during the day. Some professors teach evening or weekend classes to accommodate students who have jobs or family obligations. And some professors teach summer courses, but most use this time for conducting research, writing for publication, traveling, or professional development. Many associate and full professors are granted tenure, which means they cannot be fired without just cause or due process.

Earnings

According to the American Association of University Professors (AAUP), common salaries for college professors range from about $64,759 to $218,033. The average yearly salary, according to the AAUP, is $85,399. Earnings depend on a professor's level of education, length of service, rank and title, and disciplinary field, as well as the type of institution. Typically, wages are highest at large private research universities in New England and the Pacific Northwest and lowest at community and junior colleges in the Southeast. But even in the same institution, the salaries of professors in nonacademic fields such as medicine, engineering, business, and law generally exceed the salaries of professors in academic subjects such as philosophy, literature, history, or art.

Even in the same subject areas, salaries vary significantly based on a professor's rank. Instructors are paid less than assistant professors; assistant professors earn less than associate professors; and associate professors earn less than full professors. In addition, many universities employ part-time or adjunct professors. These individuals are usually paid per course. The AAUP reports that the median per-course wages for adjunct professors range from $1,800 to $5,225. Most full-time professors receive employee benefits that include health insurance, retirement benefits, paid sick days and vacations, and tuition discounts for dependents. Some also receive stipends for research-related travel. Adjunct professors usually do not receive benefits.

Opportunities for Advancement

Professors advance through the ranks from instructors to assistant professors to associate professors to full professors. Professors can further advance to department chairs, deans, and college presidents. Promotions are generally based on a professors' research, publications, awards, and teaching record. Professors are hired for tenure-track or nontenure-track positions. Tenure track positions afford job security because professors who obtain tenure typically cannot be dismissed from their job without a significant reason. The granting of tenure is usually based on a review of the candidate's research, contribution to the institution, and teaching. Gaining tenure can take up to seven years. However, many colleges and universities are reducing the number of tenure track positions because of the inability to fire or lay off tenured professors during uncertain economic times.

Professors who want to work in a nonacademic environment can use their knowledge and skills working for government agencies, private businesses, and research facilities. These institutions commonly afford focused research and hands-on problem solving to educators who prefer these types of environments.

What Is the Future Outlook for College Professors?

The BLS reports that between 2012 and 2022, employment for college professors is estimated to grow by 19 percent, which is faster than average for all occupations. Positions in certain subject areas are predicted to grow by up to 36 percent. These include health specialty fields such as dentistry, medicine, and laboratory technology. An expected increase in student enrollment in colleges and universities should fuel job growth in all subject areas.

Find Out More

American Association of University Professors (AAUP)
1012 Fourteenth St. NW, Suite 500
Washington, DC 20005-2029
phone: (202) 737-5900
e-mail: aaup@aaup.org
website: www.aaup.org

The AAUP provides information about issues concerning professors, including salary surveys and news and journal articles.

American Federation of Teachers (AFT)—Higher Education Division
555 New Jersey Ave. NW
Washington, DC 20001-2029
phone: (202) 879-4400
e-mail: online@aft.org
website: www.aft.org/higher_ed

The AFT Higher Education Division is a labor union representing higher education faculty and staff. It provides reports, publications, blogs, and news on issues concerning higher education faculty, students, and staff.

National Association of Scholars (NAS)
8 W. Thirty-Eighth St., Suite 503
New York, NY 10018
phone: (917) 551-6770
e-mail: contact@nas.org
website: www.nas.org

The NAS is involved in improving higher education. Among its resources are information about America's top colleges, grants and financial aid, video interviews, and publications.

National Education Association (NEA)—Higher Education Division
1201 Sixteenth St. NW
Washington, DC 20036
phone: (202) 833-4000
website: www.nea.org/he

Membership in the NEA Higher Education Division is open to post-secondary faculty and college students. Student members have access to grant opportunities, opportunities to serve on national committees, and publications.

Curriculum Developer

Curriculum developers design and develop curriculum, instructional strategies, and assessment activities for school districts based on state and national standards. They assist teachers in implementing curriculum and new teaching methods, and they serve as resource people for teachers and administrators. Most curriculum developers specialize in a subject area such as language arts, math, social studies, world languages, special education, or science. Some specialize in the development of curricula for specific grade levels, such as early childhood specialists or elementary education specialists. These educational professionals are also known as curriculum specialists, curriculum coordinators, instructional coaches, or instructional coordinators.

Although there are many aspects to these educators' job, almost everything they do is aimed at achieving one goal—enhancing student learning and achievement. One of the ways they do this is by analyzing the school district's instructional materials to make sure the cur-

At a Glance:

Curriculum Developer

Minimum Educational Requirements
Master's degree

Personal Qualities
Leadership skills
Ability to write well

Certification and Licensing
Teacher's license
School administrator credential

Working Conditions
Indoors in schools and school district offices

Salary Range
From about $33,520 to about $93,840

Number of Jobs
As of 2014 about 147,000

Future Job Outlook
Better than average

riculum correlates with state and national guidelines. If they find any discrepancies, they update the district's curriculum models and develop new material, instructional strategies, and assessment tools to better match new standards. This is important because standardized test questions are based on these standards. If students are not familiar with the required material, they are likely to perform poorly on standardized tests, which can impact whether a student passes a course or graduates. As Hillsborough, North Carolina, curriculum director/specialist Steven Weber explains on the Association for Supervision and Curriculum Development (ASCD) website, "Curriculum development is the heart of education. . . . When curriculum is misunderstood or not aligned, it has a detrimental effect on student achievement."

Another way curriculum developers boost students' academic success is by analyzing standardized test scores in an effort to pinpoint school-wide and district-wide areas of weaknesses. Once these have been identified, curriculum developers investigate ways to rectify the problem. Doing so may involve purchasing special equipment or instructional programs that target the area of weakness and training teachers in their use. Or it may involve creating new materials and teaching methods aimed at strengthening the area of weakness. In developing materials and instructional strategies, these education professionals consider many things, including how to reach students with different learning styles. For example, if students are weak in vocabulary, the language arts curriculum developer might create vocabulary-building word puzzles aimed at visual learners, vocabulary rhymes for auditory learners, and a vocabulary scavenger hunt for students who learn best through movement. To ensure that these tools are used effectively, the curriculum developer trains teachers on how to add these activities to their lessons. Curriculum developers also instruct teachers in curriculum changes, new instructional strategies, new classroom procedures, and the use of new instructional materials, technology, and teaching aids. Such sessions are often held after school. Or curriculum developers may take over scheduled classes during school hours in order to demonstrate new teaching methods while teachers observe. Indeed, mentoring teachers is an important part of the job.

These educators also assist administrators by observing teachers in their assigned subject area to evaluate performance and recommend changes that could strengthen teaching skills. They often plan and supervise special events such as academic bowls, essay contests, math nights, and spelling bees. Another important part of their work is keeping up with new developments in their subject area, as well as new ideas in curriculum and instruction. To do so, specialists attend conferences and training sessions given by publishers and makers of new technology, and they read professional journals and educational studies. Furthermore, they may travel to other school districts to observe new instructional strategies being implemented.

How Do You Become a Curriculum Developer?

Education

To prepare for a career as a curriculum developer, high school students should take classes that prepare them for college. Classes in language arts and speech are especially helpful. They prepare candidates for writing curriculum and speaking in front of large groups. A master's degree in a specialty teaching field such as secondary mathematics or in curriculum and development, educational technology, school administration, or another education major is usually the minimum requirement for this job. This entails four years of higher education to earn a bachelor's degree in education, followed by one to two years to acquire a master's degree.

Graduate-level courses typically include classes in multimedia instructional design, psychology of learning, evaluating instruction, curriculum theory, and educational administration, as well as content-specific classes that are determined by the student's subject area. Such classes are aimed at enhancing the student's content knowledge and skills and might include a class in current research in issues surrounding reading and literacy for language arts specialists or diagnosing students' mathematical thinking processes for math specialists. Those hoping to become curriculum developers can also opt to take classes that focus on elementary or secondary school or on special populations like second language learners.

Certification and Licensing

Licensing and certification requirements for curriculum developers vary by state. Most school districts require curriculum developers to have completed three to five years of successful teaching before being considered for a position as a curriculum developer. Therefore, curriculum developers should have a valid teacher's license. To obtain a teacher's license, individuals must earn a bachelor's degree from an accredited education program and successfully complete student teaching, a basic skills exam, and a content-specific exam. Many school districts require curriculum specialists to have a school administrator credential, too. Depending on the state, this credential may be general or it may be for curriculum and program administration. To obtain a school administrator's license, individuals must earn a master's degree in educational administration or in a related subject that includes a specific number of educational administration courses. Some, but not all, states require candidates for a school administrator credential to successfully complete a supervised internship or a qualifying exam.

Volunteer Work and Internships

Individuals interested in a career as a curriculum developer can gain valuable knowledge and experience by doing a variety of volunteer activities. Volunteering in a school, for example, provides prospective instructional coordinators with experience working with children and gives them a chance to learn about curriculum and instruction. Tutoring adults or children provides a similar experience. Many schools recruit community members to serve on committees such as a campus improvement committee. Doing so is another way to learn more about the workings of a school and about curriculum.

Serving on student councils is also useful. These activities help develop the type of leadership, decision making, and interpersonal skills that are needed to succeed as an instructional leader. Working on school publications, too, is helpful. It is a good way for individuals to develop and improve writing skills.

Doing a paid or voluntary internship for an educational publisher is another way to learn about curriculum and hone writing skills. Many colleges help place students in internship positions.

Finally, job shadowing a curriculum specialist for at least one day is another way to learn about the job.

Skills and Personality

Individuals with successful teaching experience who have excellent communication skills, enjoy writing, and are experts in curriculum and instruction are good candidates for curriculum developers. They should also be imaginative and like instructing others. It takes creativity to develop curriculum and instructional strategies. Creativity is also an asset in designing training sessions that engage teachers. In addition, trainers who are positive, enthusiastic, and energetic are more likely to connect with their audience.

Being analytical and a good problem solver are other important characteristics of a successful curriculum developer. These educators must be able to read, understand, and evaluate state and federal education guidelines in order to establish whether the local curriculum meets the required standards. Once this is done, they must come up with and assess various options to rectify any inconsistencies. This takes a logical mind and problem-solving skills.

In addition, these professionals must keep up with changes in education and be knowledgeable about and comfortable with technology. Other important assets include being organized, confident, and in possession of leadership skills. And, since a large part of this career involves working with people, these professionals need good interpersonal skills. They should enjoy working as part of a team and get along well with others. On occasion, instructional coordinators must deliver constructive criticism to the teachers and administrators they work with. Being pleasant and tactful can make all the difference in how this criticism is received.

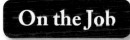

On the Job

Employers

According to the BLS, most curriculum developers are employed by public K–12 school districts and private schools. Some are employed by colleges and universities, government agencies such as state departments of education, or educational support service organizations like private tutoring services.

Working Conditions

Curriculum developers usually maintain an office in the school district's headquarters. However, they are expected to visit schools frequently. Therefore, they spend part of most workdays in transit. Generally, they are paid a mileage stipend but must provide their own transportation. Unlike teachers, they usually work year-round. They also may work evenings supervising district-wide events like art or science fairs. Vacation time varies depending on the school district. Typically, they have two to four weeks of vacation in the summer.

Earnings

The BLS reports that annual salaries for most curriculum developers range from about $35,000 to about $93,840. According to the BLS, the average median salary is $63,070. Pay depends on the location of the job and the educators' level of education, length of service, and training. As of April 1, 2014, the BLS reports the following places with the highest mean annual wage for curriculum developers: District of Columbia, $77,620; Connecticut, $75,830; New Jersey, $74,530; California, $72,560; and Colorado, $69,460. In addition, these education professionals generally receive employee benefits, including health insurance, retirement benefits, and paid sick days and vacations.

Opportunities for Advancement

Curriculum developers with a school administrator credential can advance to higher administrative positions such as school principal, director of curriculum and instruction, program director, assistant superintendent, or superintendent. With a doctoral degree, they can advance to college professorships. They can also leave the education sector and become textbook authors or editors or curriculum developers for educational publishers, software companies, or corporate training programs. Their training and leadership experience also makes them good candidates for positions as corporate managers.

What Is the Future Outlook for Curriculum Developers?

The BLS estimates that employment for curriculum developers will grow 13 percent between 2012 and 2022, which is faster than average for all occupations. The growing focus on holding school districts, individual schools, and teachers accountable for student achievement is expected to increase demand for these professionals. With states, the federal government, and school districts using various accountability measures, including standardized test scores and student graduation rates, curriculum developers will be needed to improve and evaluate curriculum and provide training and mentoring for teachers so they can meet accountability standards.

Find Out More

Association for Supervision and Curriculum Development (ASCD)
1703 N. Beauregard St.
Alexandria, VA 22311-1714
phone: 800-933-ASCD (2723)
fax: 703-575-5400
website: www.ascd.org

The ASCD produces publications, conferences, and online tools about teaching, learning, curriculum development, national education standards, and educational leadership.

Big Future by the College Board
website: https://bigfuture.collegeboard.org

This website provides career profiles for many careers. Its instructional coordinators' page gives information about the job and how to prepare for it.

Education Careers Review
website: http://education-careers-review.toptenreviews.com

This website lists the top ten education careers for 2014 and provides information about each career, including that of a curriculum developer.

Education Portal
website: http://education-portal.com

This website compiles information about various careers, including that of a curriculum specialist. It describes the job, education and training needed, and related careers.

International Reading Association
800 Barksdale Road
PO Box 8139
Newark, DE 19714-8139
phone (800) 336-7323
website: www.reading.org

The International Reading Association promotes worldwide literacy. Its website provides state and federal language arts standards and information about reading instruction. It offers workshops, conferences, and professional journals.

Early Childhood Educator

Early childhood educators teach and care for children who have not yet been to kindergarten. Different early childhood educators work with different age groups; pupils range in age from infancy through five years old, with the majority of students aged three to five. Also known as early childhood teachers or preschool teachers, these educators help youngsters develop physically, socially, and emotionally. They use games, songs, storytelling, and other creative and fun activities to stimulate their young students' natural curiosity and imagination and to develop their communication and problem-solving skills. Some of these educators might specialize in working with children with physical, emotional, or learning disabilities.

Early childhood teachers have an active day. Even before the students arrive, these professionals are busy getting

At a Glance:
Early Childhood Educator

Minimum Educational Requirements
High school diploma

Personal Qualities
Energetic
Nurturing

Certification and Licensing
Child Development Associate Credential

Working Conditions
Indoors in schools and child care centers

Salary Range
From about $18,420 to $49,660

Number of Jobs
As of 2014 about 438,200

Future Outlook
Better than average

Guided by their teacher, preschool children learn to express themselves with colorful paints. They might be painting a scene from a story, depicting an activity from their day, or portraying an imagined creature or event.

learning centers such as sand tables, play areas, puppet stages, painting and drawing centers, and library corners ready for students. The educators design each center to make sure they provide children with a variety of learning experiences. As Pennsylvania preschool teacher Trish Nodolski explains in an interview on the Teacher Certification Degrees website, "We may set up a [mock] grocery store, pet shop, post office, or hot chocolate store where the children can write, do math, compare, use manners and organize."

Once the school day begins, preschool teachers greet parents as they drop off students, welcome their young pupils, and help them take off their outerwear. Often, class begins with the early childhood teacher leading the children in a daily salutation that includes a song of greetings, a sharing event such as show and tell, and a discussion about the calendar. The educator may then break the children up into play groups, assigning each group to a different learning area. As the children play, the teacher moves among the groups, monitoring the children and encouraging them to interact with each other. This activity may be followed by snack time, which the teacher oversees and uses as an opportunity to instruct the children in how to eat properly and clean up after themselves. Then there will likely be a supervised nap time. Depending on the children's age, the teacher may take them outside to the playground for recess or for a supervised game. The rest of the instructional day may include the teacher using puppets to teach important concepts, reading the children a story, and leading them in songs and finger plays.

These activities are rarely impromptu. Early childhood educators plan for each day. They establish a flexible daily routine, which helps young children feel more secure, and employ curriculum that targets different areas of child development. At the same time, they make sure that schedules and routines allow for children to have adequate physical activity, rest, and playtime.

Teaching children is only part of the job. These professionals often take on parental responsibilities, too. Those who work with infants and the youngest children change diapers and bottle-feed their charges. And, because being away from home and family can be scary for youngsters, especially at the beginning of the school year, these educators often spend a lot of time soothing anxious students and wiping away tears. They also work closely with parents, reassuring them about leaving their children, as well as keeping parents informed on their child's progress and on problems that may arise.

How Do You Become an Early Childhood Educator?

Education

Some high schools offer a career or technical program in early childhood education. Participating in such a program is a good way to pre-

27

pare for a career as an early childhood teacher. Students who do not have access to this type of program can prepare for this career by taking classes on child development, which provide candidates with an understanding of how youngsters grow. Classes in speech, art, music, and drama help individuals develop the confidence and the skills they need to lead youngsters in artistic activities. If an individual plans to work in an area of the country in which many people do not speak English, studying a foreign language, especially Spanish, is helpful. Specific education requirements for this profession vary widely depending on the state and the school or child care program. At a minimum, early childhood educators must be high school graduates. They then receive on-the-job training. In addition, some programs require preschool educators to have first aid and CPR training in case any of their students need basic medical assistance. Many states, private preschools, and early childhood programs require educators to have a two-year associate's degree in early childhood development or a four-year bachelor's degree in early childhood education. The latter prepares students to teach preschool through third grade. As an example of how diverse requirements for this career are, Texas does not require any degree or special training, whereas New Jersey requires a bachelor's degree. Federally funded Head Start programs require that at least 50 percent of Head Start teachers have a bachelor's degree, whereas others receive on-the-job training. Although postsecondary education may not be required for all positions in this field, it increases a candidate's employability and opportunities for advancement.

Postsecondary course work for both an associate's and a bachelor's degree focuses on the intellectual development of young children. Course work includes supervised field experience and, for bachelor's degree candidates, a semester of student teaching.

Certification and Licensing

As with educational requirements, certification and licensing requirements vary by state, program, and school. Many states require preschool teachers to have a Child Development Associate (CDA) credential, which is awarded by the Council for Professional Recognition. Candidates for the credential must have graduated from high school and completed 120 credit or noncredit hours of early childhood education training, which can be obtained through an institution or organization with expertise in early childhood education, such as a community college, nanny school, community agency, or professional organization. In addition, candidates must have completed 480 hours of work experience with young children within the previous three years and be observed by a CDA specialist, who assesses the candidate's competency.

Early childhood educators employed in prekindergarten programs in public schools must have a valid teacher's license. To obtain one, candidates must have a bachelor's degree from an accredited education program and have successfully completed a term of student teaching, a written basic skills exam, and a written exam specific to early childhood education.

Volunteer Work and Internships

Working part time or volunteering in a day care center, preschool, kindergarten, or other child care program is a good way for individuals to test whether they like working with young children. Such activities also help prospective preschool teachers learn more about the career. Babysitting or working in summer camps are other ways to get experience working with children; so is volunteering to read aloud during story time at a library or a bookstore.

Doing an internship that involves working with infants or young children is another way to gain valuable experience. Many colleges and universities offer students opportunities for an internship, employment, or volunteer work in campus-based preschools and child care centers. Often, students receive college credit for serving in these facilities. College departments of education help match early childhood education majors with off-campus internship opportunities in facilities such as schools, day care centers, community centers, social agencies, and private businesses with child care facilities.

Skills and Personality

Early childhood educators should enjoy working with young children and be knowledgeable about child development. Although every child develops at a different pace, there are certain developmental milestones specific to certain ages. Preschool teachers need to understand what these are in order to plan age-appropriate activities that do not frustrate young students. And, because young children are quite sensitive and cry easily, these professionals should be caring and nurturing. Preschoolers can also be unruly, loud, irritable, and irrational. Patience goes a long way in dealing with such behavior.

These educators should also be physically fit. It takes a lot of energy to keep up with this age group. Teachers are on their feet most of the day. They also lift and carry infants and toddlers and help students dress and undress. They clean up messes when children soil themselves, spill things, and get sick. Exposure to germs and a variety of illnesses is common. These professionals cannot be squeamish.

In addition, preschool teachers must be alert. Failing to keep watch on these youngsters even for a few minutes can lead to disaster. Other important character traits that help individuals succeed in this career include being organized, energetic, and dedicated to helping children. Moreover, since these professionals spend a lot of time dealing with parents, they should be tactful and have good communication and interpersonal skills.

On the Job

Employers

The BLS reports that 54 percent of preschool teachers are employed by child day care services. Others are employed by private preschools and public prekindergarten programs. Some also work for religious, social, charitable, and civic organizations, individual and family services, and private businesses that offer child care services. A few childhood educators are self-employed, owning and operating day care facilities or preschools.

Working Conditions

Preschools and day care facilities are usually colorful, noisy places. Depending on the facility, they can be spacious or crowded. Class sizes vary. In most cases the child-to-adult ratio is regulated by the state. Generally, one teacher may be responsible for six to eight babies or ten to twenty older children. These professionals spend much of the time indoors but also are responsible for supervising children as they play outdoors.

Teachers' work schedules depend on the needs of the facility. In order to accommodate working parents, some facilities are open from early morning to 6:00 or 7:00 p.m., year-round. Other programs follow public school hours and vacation schedules. And since some children do not attend preschool all day, schools might have a morning and an afternoon session. In some cases teachers instruct both sessions. In other cases educators are employed part-time. Part-time early childhood educators work between fifteen and thirty hours per week. Full-time teachers work between thirty-five and forty hours per week.

Earnings

Preschool teachers typically earn less than elementary or secondary school teachers. Pay depends on the school or child care facility and the teacher's education level, training, and experience. The BLS reports an annual mean salary for early childhood educators of $27,570, with the average mean wages highest in the following states: New York, $43,350; New Jersey, $36,970; Kentucky, $36,750; Alaska, $35,980; Connecticut $34,520. It reports that most salaries range from about $18,420 to $49,660. Full-time early childhood educators usually receive employee benefits that include health insurance, retirement benefits, and paid sick and vacation days. Part-time employees usually do not receive any benefits.

Opportunities for Advancement

Early childhood teachers' salaries usually increase with advanced training, education, and experience. Educators with experience and a bachelor's degree can advance to a position of head or lead teacher or into an administrative position as a preschool director. Those with a valid teacher's license and a credential in early childhood education can work as a prekindergarten to third grade teacher in a public school, where salaries are generally higher than in private facilities. A master's or doctoral degree qualifies individuals to teach in college and university early childhood education programs. Some early childhood educators start their own preschool programs.

What Is the Future Outlook for Early Childhood Educators?

The BLS estimates that employment for early childhood educators will grow by 17 percent between 2012 and 2022, which is faster than average. One reason for this growth is the increasing emphasis on young children's intellectual and social development. Another is that the population of three- to five-year-old children is expected to grow, increasing the demand for preschool teachers.

Find Out More

Council for Professional Recognition
2460 Sixteenth St. NW
Washington, DC 20009-3575
phone: (800) 424-4310
website: www.cdacouncil.org

The Council for Professional Recognition provides information about obtaining a CDA credential, including lists of training schools and organizations, CDA specialists, and exam sites.

Education Portal
website: http://education-portal.com

This website provides information about a wide range of careers. The section on preschool teachers offers information about the job, salary, and education requirements.

National Association for the Education of Young Children (NAEYC)
1509 Sixteenth St. NW
Washington, DC 20036-1426
phone: (800) 424-2460
website: www.naeyc.org

The NAEYC is the world's largest organization representing the welfare of young children. It provides a wealth of information on teaching young children, many publications, and lists of early childhood education associate's and bachelor's degree programs.

PreSchool Education.com
website: www.preschooleducation.com

This website provides all sorts of activities and ideas that would be helpful to preschool teachers, volunteers, and interns. It also offers articles and information about developmental milestones.

Education Administrator

Education administrators manage and provide leadership in schools. They fill a variety of roles. In elementary and secondary schools they serve as principals, assistant principals, and school district administrators. In postsecondary schools, they serve as deans, directors, and college presidents. Although the duties of these professionals vary depending on the specific job, the primary goal of all education administrators is to keep schools running smoothly so that all students receive the best education possible.

Administrators achieve this goal in a variety of ways. School principals, for instance, serve as school managers and instructional leaders. They are responsible for everything that goes on in a school. Besides overseeing the day-to-day operations of the school, they serve as instructional leaders who are responsible for student and faculty performance. In an article on the

At a Glance:
Education Administrator

Minimum Educational Requirements
Master's degree

Personal Qualities
Leadership and managerial skills
Interpersonal skills

Certification and Licensing
Teacher's license
School administrator credential

Working Conditions
K–12 schools, school district offices, colleges, and universities

Salary Range
From about $49,660 to $171,040

Number of Jobs
As of 2014 about 393,300

Future Job Outlook
Varies by position

website EducationWorld, Amos Kornfeld, the principal at Piermont Village School in New Hampshire, describes his job in the following way: "I visit classrooms regularly, provide feedback for teachers, introduce initiatives . . . hire good people and help lose poor teachers, create a culture of high expectations and caring, [and] facilitate shared decision-making."

Assistant principals help the principal, performing many of the same duties as the principal. District administrators, too, support principals. They direct different instructional and noninstructional programs. Instructional directors manage curriculum and special programs such as vocational education, special education, and bilingual education. Noninstructional directors supervise programs that support schools, like food service, transportation, security, and custodial services.

School superintendents and college presidents are chief executive officers of school districts and postsecondary schools. In a large school district or at a university, these executives oversee hundreds of employees, a student body of several thousands, and budgets that may exceed $100 million. They manage issues such as student achievement, instructional and noninstructional services, budgets, general operations, and relations with government agencies, local businesses, the public, and the media. As Conestoga Valley, Pennsylvania, school superintendent Gerald Huesken told *LancasterOnline*, "[The job] extends beyond the leadership role for an education organization to other areas, such as meeting regularly with our state legislators to lobby for public education, networking with community groups and creating alternative revenue sources."

Superintendents are assisted by assistant superintendents. College presidents are assisted by directors and deans, among other administrators. There are different types of college deans. Academic deans supervise a group of departments that form a "school" or "college" at a university, such as the dean of the School of Education or the dean of the College of Engineering. Like a school principal, these administrators are responsible for everything that goes on in their school. They are involved in recruiting and hiring faculty, coordinating course scheduling, setting and enforcing academic and institutional policies, and developing and managing the budget. Other deans, known as deans of students, are in charge of student affairs. They work with various partners on a college campus to provide and connect students with out-of-classroom programs and services that enhance learning. These programs include financial aid, housing, and student health services; career and internship programs; and student disciplinary programs, among others. They also mediate conflicts between students and faculty, help foreign students navigate the laws and rules specific to them, and oversee campus special events like concerts and festivals.

Directors manage specific programs. For example, athletic directors are in charge of all college sports programs. They hire and oversee coaches and athletic staff, and they manage the athletic department's budget and supervise the maintenance of athletic facilities, among other duties. Other directors supervise admission procedures, student organizations and activities, and campus safety.

How Do You Become an Education Administrator?

Education

High school students interested in becoming education administrators should take classes that prepare them for college. Classes in math are especially useful since these professionals administer and prepare budgets. Courses in speech and language arts help, too. These classes prepare future education administrators to speak before large groups and write reports to document student achievement and compliance with state and federal regulations, for example. Education administrators must have a minimum of a master's degree in educational administration or a related field. It usually takes four years beyond high school to earn a bachelor's degree, and one to two additional years to earn a master's degree. A doctoral degree is usually required for a position as a dean, college president, or school superintendent.

Graduate-level courses include classes in educational leadership, school finance, school law, higher education administration, and in some cases field experience or a supervised internship.

Certification and Licensing

Certification and licensing requirements vary depending on the specific job. Postsecondary administrators do not need any licenses or certificates. School administrators, however, do. Generally, school administrators are required to have a teacher's license and a school administrator credential. To obtain a school administrator credential, candidates must earn a master's degree in educational administration or in a subject other than educational administration that includes a specific number of educational administration courses. Some, but not all, states require candidates for a school administrator to successfully complete a supervised internship or a qualifying exam.

Volunteer Work and Internships

Individuals interested in a career as an education administrator can gain valuable knowledge about the job by following an education administrator in the candidate's field of interest through a workday. Individuals can also gain insight and experience by doing a variety of volunteer or intern activities. Volunteering or serving as an intern in a school's front office, in the office of a dean, or in the central office of a school district gives individuals a chance to observe educational administrators in action. Individuals might also volunteer in a school as an aide, tutor, or coach or assistant coach with a youth sports team. These positions give candidates experience working with and leading young people. Serving on student council or a dormitory leadership team, as the captain of a sports team, or as the chair of a school or club committee is also useful. Such activities help develop the type of managerial, decision-making, and interpersonal skills that are needed to succeed as an administrator.

Skills and Personality

Education administrators are managers. To do their job effectively, they need excellent leadership and team-building skills. These professionals serve as team leaders and must be able to get the best out of every member of their educational team. Being personable, tactful, and confident helps them do so, as does being respectful and tolerant of different types of people. And since an administrator is often the face and voice of a school, university, district, or special program, good interpersonal skills are also essential in dealing with the media and community members. Having good listening, speaking, and writing skills is also important. Such skills help administrators listen to and clearly respond to the concerns of students, parents, staff, and community members, as well as write reports.

Other important attributes include being detail oriented, organized, logical, decisive, and a good problem solver. Even with the best preparation, school operations and programs do not always go as planned, and crises often arise. Administrators must be able to come up with on-the-spot solutions in order to solve unexpected problems. They should also be computer literate and, in order to develop budgets and analyze data, must be comfortable working with statistics and numbers.

To become administrators, individuals typically must have prior experience in teaching. Principals, assistant principals, and instructional directors usually must have a minimum of three years' previous successful teaching experience. Similarly, superintendents and assistant superintendents usually must have previous experience as principals. Academic deans must have served successfully as a college professor. And postsecondary directors, deans of students, and college presidents are required to have previous management experience in the field they direct. This helps ensure that these administrative personnel have familiarity with the demands and constraints of teaching so that they can effectively relate to faculty members and quickly comprehend their concerns and needs.

On the Job

Employers
Education administrators are employed by public and private schools, colleges and universities, technical institutes, and other postsecondary facilities.

Working Conditions
Administrators work in schools and colleges. They usually have a private office and an executive assistant or secretary assigned to them. They work at least forty hours per week, year-round. Working eve-

nings, nights, and weekends and attending student activities, school functions, meetings, fund-raising events, and professional conferences are part of the job. They also often work late completing reports and other important paperwork. Vacation time depends on the position and the employer.

Education administrative positions are stressful. Professionals in these positions are held accountable for their school or program's successes and failures. They must also make sure that the programs they oversee meet federal and state guidelines for funding; student attendance, graduation, and performance; and teacher qualifications. Funding shortfalls due to economic slowdowns put pressure on these leaders, too.

Earnings

Earnings vary depending on the position. The BLS reports that elementary and secondary administrators' wages range from $59,010 to $128,110. It reports a mean annual wage of $90,670. School superintendents are the highest-paid school administrator in this group, and their earnings are typically in the top 10 percent of the pay scale.

According to the BLS, postsecondary administrators' wages range from $49,660 to $171,040. It reports a mean annual salary of $100,600. College presidents are the highest-paid postsecondary administrators. Their earnings are typically in the top 10 percent of the given range.

Typically, education administrators receive employee benefits that include health insurance, retirement benefits, and paid sick and vacation days. School superintendents and college presidents often are given use of an automobile. Some college presidents are given housing during their employment.

Opportunities for Advancement

Elementary and secondary school principals and assistant principals can advance to district-level administrators. Postsecondary administrators can also work their way up the administrative ladder. Preference is usually given to candidates with a doctoral degree. In both school and college administration, each increase in job responsibility coincides with a salary increase. With their managerial and leadership experience, education administrators can also advance to managerial and executive positions in private industry, public agencies, and government.

What Is the Future Outlook for Education Administrators?

The future outlook for education administrators varies depending on the position. The BLS estimates that employment for elementary and secondary administrators will grow by 6 percent between 2012 and 2022, which is slower than average. However, a large portion of current school administrators are expected to retire within the next ten years. As these men and women leave the profession, their jobs will need to be filled. Opportunities also vary by region. Job growth is expected to be greatest in states where the population is growing fastest, such as Texas, Utah, Colorado, North Dakota, Nevada, and South Dakota. School administrators are also in greater demand in rural and urban areas.

The BLS predicts that estimated employment during the same time period for postsecondary administrators will grow by 15 percent, which is greater than average. An expected increase in student enrollment in colleges, universities, and technical institutes should fuel this growth.

Find Out More

American Association of School Superintendents (AASA)
1615 Duke St.
Alexandria, VA 22314
phone: (703) 528-0700
e-mail: info@aasa.org
website: www.aasa.org

The AASA is a professional organization of school superintendents and other educational leaders. It provides information, publications, and conferences on issues affecting education administrators.

American Association of University Administrators (AAUA)
214 Meadville St.
Edinboro, PA 16412
phone: (814) 460-6498
e-mail: dking@aaua.org
website: www.aaua.org

The AAUA publishes a journal, sponsors awards, and holds leadership seminars. Membership, which is open to postsecondary administrators and students preparing for careers in the field, provides networking opportunities.

National Association of Elementary School Principals
1615 Duke St.
Alexandria, VA 22314
phone: (800) 386-2377
e-mail: naesp@naesp.org
website: www.naesp.org

This national association provides information on issues involving elementary and middle school administration, including publications, conferences, online learning, and certification.

National Association of Secondary School Principals (NASSP)
1904 Association Dr.
Reston, VA 20191-1537
phone: (703) 860-0200
website: www.principals.org

This organization provides information about issues affecting secondary school administrators. It also sponsors a number of student programs aimed at developing student leaders.

K–12 Teacher

K–12 teachers (elementary and secondary teachers) instruct students in elementary, middle, and high schools. Elementary schools comprise kindergarten through grades five or six. Middle schools comprise grades six or seven through grade eight, and high schools comprise grades nine through twelve. In most states elementary teachers are licensed to instruct students in kindergarten through grade eight. Some states also have a certificate for grades four through eight, which licenses individuals to teach upper elementary school and middle school. Secondary teachers are licensed to instruct students in grades seven through twelve. Therefore, elementary teachers work in elementary and middle schools, whereas secondary teachers work in middle and high schools.

Elementary teachers may instruct the same group of students in all academic subjects, or they may be responsible for teaching one academic subject to students in a particular grade level, such as a sixth-grade science teacher. Some elementary teachers specialize in teaching

At a Glance:
K–12 Teacher

Minimum Educational Requirements
Bachelor's degree

Personal Qualities
Patient
Organized

Certification and Licensing
Teacher's license with certification in elementary or secondary education

Working Conditions
In schools

Salary Range
From about $35,760 to $86,720

Number of Jobs
As of 2014 about 2,912,940

Future Outlook
Better than average for elementary and middle school teachers; below average for high school teachers

art, music, physical education, or computer science to students in multiple grade levels. These specialists have the unique opportunity to watch their students grow and change over a number of years.

Secondary teachers specialize in a specific subject. Areas of specialization include traditional academic subjects, the fine arts, computer science, or physical education, as well as more-specialized vocational subjects. Each secondary teacher is responsible for teaching that subject to one or more grade levels. For instance, a high school mathematics teacher may teach Algebra I to ninth graders, geometry to tenth graders, trigonometry to eleventh graders, and precalculus to twelfth graders.

Depending on the grade level and subject area, in a typical day K–12 teachers instruct anywhere from twenty to more than one hundred students. Generally, elementary school teachers instruct fewer students than middle and high school teachers. In addition to providing subject matter instruction, K–12 teachers help students develop study, thinking, test-taking, and social skills. The last often involves helping students learn how to behave in school and how to get along with others.

Although the main part of their job is instructing youngsters, K–12 teachers perform a variety of other duties. In an interview on the Teacher Certification Degrees website, Megan Favre, a Texas third-grade language arts teacher, describes a typical school day in this way: "The simple version has me teaching reading, writing, and working with small groups while my [other] students work independently. . . . The real life version also involves meetings, e-mails, solving disagreements, fire drills, addressing behavior issues, tending to a sick or injured child, forgetting something I needed to do, and then finally laughing about it all at the end of the school day."

How Do You Become a K–12 Teacher?

Education

To prepare for a career as an elementary or secondary teacher, individuals in high school should take classes that ready them for college. If a prospective teacher plans to work in an area of the country where many people do not speak English, studying a foreign language, especially Spanish, is helpful.

All K–12 teachers must have a minimum of a bachelor's degree from an accredited teacher education program. Many go on to earn a master's degree, which enhances opportunities for advancement. Depending on the university and the state, students can either major in education with twenty-four to thirty-six credits in a specific subject, or they can major in a specific subject and take twenty-four to thirty-six credits in education.

Course work for all K–12 educators includes required liberal arts and science classes, subject area classes, and education classes. The latter give candidates insights into the fundamentals of learning and instruction. As part of their education, students visit classrooms and observe teachers in action. Before graduating, candidates get real experience through fieldwork and a semester of student teaching under the guidance of an experienced teacher.

Certification and Licensing

All fifty states and the District of Columbia require elementary and secondary teachers employed by public schools to be licensed. Licensing requirements vary by state. College education departments can advise students about licensing requirements for the state in which the college is located. Many states practice license reciprocity. This allows educators to transfer their license between states. In general, to become licensed, candidates must earn a bachelor's degree from an accredited education program, successfully complete a semester of student teaching, and pass a written basic skills exam and a written exam specific to elementary school teaching or specific to a particular subject area for secondary school. Licensing requirements for private and parochial schools vary.

Some states allow unlicensed individuals with a bachelor's degree to teach while completing an accelerated education program under alternative certification programs.

Volunteer Work and Internships

Volunteering to work with children, young adolescents, or teens gives individuals a chance to see whether they like working with a particular age group, as well as experience instructing groups of young people. Volunteer positions can be found in schools, community centers, scout troops, and church youth groups. Doing peer tutoring or working in a summer camp are other good ways for individuals to test whether they enjoy instructing others.

Doing an internship is another excellent method of gaining experience and knowledge about teaching. Many college education departments maintain a database of paid and unpaid internship opportunities and help match students with positions that best suit their career goals. For instance, the University of California–Davis helps place students into internships as teacher's aides in local public schools. This gives participants an excellent opportunity to spend time in a classroom working closely with students and teachers. Similarly, job shadowing a teacher is another way to learn more about the job.

Skills and Personality

K–12 teachers are role models for students. What these educators say and do may have a lasting impact on those whom they teach. Therefore, successful elementary and secondary teachers are conscious of how their behavior, words, and attitudes affect their students. They are tolerant of people of different cultures and respectful of their students as individuals, showing a real interest in their success in life. For example, many teachers give their students a card with a handwritten note on their birthdays. Small acts like this help students feel supported and valued—and therefore more motivated to learn.

Patience, understanding, self-discipline, and fairness are also essential character traits. Students do not always respond the way teachers hope. They may act out, perform poorly, or seem uninterested in school. This can be frustrating for teachers. Educators must be able to control their own emotions, show patience and understanding, and be consistent in the way they handle behavioral issues. The latter involves making students aware of rules and consequences and consistently enforcing them without showing favoritism.

In addition, teachers should have good communication skills so they can clearly and effectively transmit knowledge and skills to their students. And since every teacher is the head of a class, these professionals should be skilled leaders.

On the Job

Employers

Most elementary and secondary teachers are employed by public and private schools. They might also find jobs at other state educational institutions, juvenile detention centers, or social agencies.

Working Conditions

Almost all K–12 teachers work in schools. Work conditions vary depending on the school. Most schools are pleasant and cheerful. However, some are old, overcrowded, or in poor condition. Moreover, it is not unusual for students to bring personal issues to school and for fights to break out on school grounds, which can create a tense environment.

The majority of teachers usually have their own classrooms. Some teachers, such as physical education and vocational education teachers, may also have small offices. Elementary and secondary teachers are on their feet most of the day and do a lot of talking.

Most teachers work approximately 185 to 190 days per year. Traditionally, this translates to ten months per year, with a two-month break in the summer. Those who work in schools on a nontraditional, year-round schedule typically work forty-five days in a row with fifteen days off or sixty days with twenty days off. Then the cycle begins again. Work hours are set by the local school district. A typical school day usually starts at 8:00 a.m. and ends at 3:00 p.m. Teachers may stay after hours to meet with parents, sponsor clubs, or coach sports teams. Plus they often grade papers, write lesson plans, or complete other paperwork at home.

Earnings

The BLS reports that most salaries for K–12 teachers range from about $35,760 to $86,720. Salaries depend on the location and the educators' level of education, length of service, and training. The BLS further reports a mean annual salary of $58,260 for high school teachers, $56,630 for middle school teachers, and $56,320 for elementary school teachers. Generally, salaries for all K–12 educators follow the same scale in most school districts. Average salary differences can be

A high school teacher assists a student who is working on a research paper. High school teachers spend a lot of time preparing for and giving lectures, but they also work directly with students on class assignments and research papers.

explained by the fact that middle and high school teachers are more likely than elementary school teachers to serve as department heads and coaches, for which they receive extra pay.

Most K–12 teachers receive employee benefits that include health insurance, paid sick and vacation days, and retirement benefits. In addition, the federal government will cancel up to 100 percent of federal Perkins student loans for teachers who work for one school year in a school that serves low-income students, as well as for teachers in any field of expertise in which there is a shortage of qualified teachers. Shortage areas are determined by the US Department of Education and state education agencies. As of 2014 the Department of Education has determined that bilingual education, foreign languages, math, and science are fields that are always in need of teachers. Other common shortage areas identified by a number of states include English, ESOL, special education, and vocational education, among others. The government also offers student loan forgiveness of up to $17,500 for other types of student loans for individuals who teach for five consecutive school years. In addition, many states and cities offer loan forgiveness for educators who teach in state-identified, subject-shortage areas.

Opportunities for Advancement

In most school districts teachers are paid on the basis of their years of service, education level, and performance evaluation. K–12 teachers with good performance evaluations, a master's degree or higher, and twenty or more years of service are paid at the top of the pay scale. Possessing experience and a master's degree can also advance educators to positions as department heads or curriculum specialists. A master's degree in school administration qualifies teachers to become principals, assistant principals, private school directors, and district-level administrators. Possessing a doctorate qualifies individuals to advance to faculty positions in college and university education programs. Some educators own and operate tutoring or testing services.

What Is the Future Outlook for K–12 Teachers?

The BLS estimates that employment for elementary and middle school teachers will grow by 12 percent from 2012 to 2022, which is better than average. It estimates employment for high school teachers will grow by 6 percent in the same time frame, which is less than average. However, there is currently a chronic shortage of high school teachers in certain fields, such as math, science, and world languages, with the greatest shortages in inner cities, low-income schools, and rural areas. Filling these positions with qualified educators is a top priority. Moreover, teaching can be stressful, and many teachers resign each year. Qualified professionals are needed to replace educators who leave the field.

Find Out More

American Federation of Teachers (AFT)
555 New Jersey Ave. NW
Washington, DC 20001
phone: (202) 879-4400

website: www.aft.org

The AFT is a labor union that represents 1.6 million teachers. It provides information on all issues affecting educators, including information about becoming a teacher.

Future Educators Association (FEA)
PO Box 7888
Bloomington, IN 47407-7888
phone: (800) 766-1156
e-mail: fea@pdkintl.org
website: www.futureeducators.org

The FEA is an organization for high school students interested in becoming educators. It provides information about careers in teaching, a national conference, and scholarships.

National Education Association (NEA)
1201 Sixteenth St. NW
Washington, DC 20036
phone: (202) 833-4000
website: www.nea.org

The NEA is the largest organization of professional educators in the United States. It offers information about becoming a teacher, getting a teaching job, teacher salaries, and student loans.

Teach California
website: www.teachcalifornia.org

This website is administered by the California Department of Education. It has information about a career as a K–12 teacher, including videos and interviews with teachers, types of teaching careers, and characteristics of an effective teacher.

Library Media Specialist

Library media specialists are also known as information specialists, information technologists, and school librarians. They manage school library media centers that promote literacy and provide students, faculty, and staff access to information from a wide variety of sources. These include print materials such as books and periodicals, audiovisual materials, up-to-date software, and multimedia workstations where library patrons can access digital information and do research. These professionals are trained and knowledgeable in the use of information technology and are essential to bringing the digital world into classrooms. A large part of their job is making sure that school networks extend the availability of information resources such as licensed databases beyond the library media center to classrooms and computer laboratories throughout the building.

At a Glance:
Library Media Specialist

Minimum Educational Requirements
Master's degree

Personal Qualities
Organized
Computer skills

Certification and Licensing
Teacher's license
Library media specialist credential

Working Conditions
Indoors in school library media centers

Salary Range
From about $33,380 to $86,320

Number of Jobs
As of 2014 about 156,000

Future Job Outlook
Slower than average

A library media specialist, or librarian, helps students sift through an online database or Internet source for useful information. School librarians rely on their knowledge of books and the online world to guide students in finding reading materials and completing class assignments.

These educators work to create a school environment that helps students become enthusiastic learners, readers, critical thinkers, problem solvers, and skillful researchers. With these goals in mind, library media specialists instruct groups and individual students on how to acquire, evaluate, and use information and technology to do research. They also conduct read-aloud sessions aimed at stimulating students' interest in literature. These read-aloud sessions may also serve as an introduction to a lesson that the librarian presents about a particular author or literary genre. To further encourage students to read, library media specialists invite authors to visit their schools.

These educators also serve as teacher trainers, conducting training sessions aimed at keeping educators informed about the latest information resources and technology. Moreover, they act as a resource person for teachers, assisting them in selecting and gathering print and digital materials that enhance instruction. "It's the librarian's job to assist teachers with their instructional needs," explains John Busby, a former Dallas library media specialist. "To help with the curriculum objectives of the classroom teacher, I gathered appropriate materials and worked directly with the teacher to implement the teacher's instructional goals."

Library media specialists are also responsible for budgeting, developing, and maintaining the library media center's resources. A big part of this job is purchasing materials that support the curriculum for each grade level and/or subject area. In order to develop a collection of resources appropriate to the curriculum, they research what materials are available. Then they meet with teachers to identify what materials each teacher needs to best address the curriculum, the teacher's instructional strategies, and students' diverse learning styles.

These professional educators also attend to many housekeeping tasks such as checking books and materials in and out, shelving materials, making and maintaining inventories, keeping records on material circulation, and discarding out-of-date material. In some schools librarians maintain and update the campus's web page. Gathering information from teachers, students, support staff, and administrators for the web page and making appropriate changes may also be part of a typical day. When applicable, library media specialists supervise library technicians and student aides who assist in the day-to-day operations of the library.

How Do You Become a Library Media Specialist?

Education

To prepare for a career as a library media specialist, high school students should take classes that ready them for college. Taking classes in language arts, which introduce future librarians to a variety of literature, is helpful. And since twenty-first-century school libraries are technology hubs, computer science classes are a must. Although educational requirements for this career vary by state, school district, and school, generally employers require a master's degree in library and information science. This entails four years of higher education to earn a bachelor's degree in a field that meets the requirements for a teacher's license, followed by one to two years to acquire a master's degree.

Graduate-level courses are designed to give individuals the knowledge and skills they need to manage a school library media center. Course work typically includes classes in instructional materials production and use, information organization, information resources development, library operations and policy development, and literature for youth, among other topics.

The American Library Association and state library associations offer financial assistance and scholarships to qualified candidates who want to become library media specialists. This includes a number of scholarships for minority candidates and candidates with disabilities.

Certification and Licensing

Licensing requirements for library media specialists vary by school and state. Typically, library media specialists in public schools are required to hold a valid teacher's license and a library media specialist credential. To earn a teacher's license, candidates must earn a bachelor's degree from an accredited education program, successfully complete student teaching, pass a written basic skills exam, and pass a written exam specific to a teaching field. To earn a library media specialist credential, candidates must successfully earn a master's degree from a program accredited by the American Library Association or the National Council for Accreditation of Teacher Education. Requirements for private schools vary.

Volunteer Work and Internships

Working as a volunteer in a school library media center is an excellent way to learn about this career. Many high schools offer service-learning credit to students who help in the library for one class period per day. Volunteering or working part-time in a public or college library is another good way to see what a librarian does. So is following a school librarian for a day as he or she works.

Doing an internship is another excellent method of gaining experience and knowledge about librarianship. Many college education departments maintain a database of paid and unpaid internship opportunities and help match students with positions that best suit their career goals.

Skills and Personality

Many, but not all, schools require library media specialists to have previous successful teaching experience. Indeed, having excellent teaching skills is essential to being an effective library media specialist. And because a large part of the job is integrating modern technology into classroom instruction, these professionals should have strong technology skills. This includes the ability to use database software, accounting software, Internet software, e-mail, spreadsheets, and word processing software.

Enjoying helping others and having strong interpersonal skills are also important. School librarians interact with people all day long. They work with almost every student and teacher in a school. They also interact with administrators and support staff. Many supervise library technicians and student library aides. It takes a tactful, courteous person who likes people and is a good leader to successfully deal with all these people. These professionals also need to be able to communicate effectively with others, both orally and in writing. They need to be good listeners and problem solvers so that they can help teachers and students find the best materials to suit their particular instructional and learning needs. And since they are responsible for budgeting, they should have good math skills.

Moreover, since these educators perform a variety of roles on campus, their job demands versatility. In an article on the Scholastic website, Don Knezek, chief executive officer of the International Society for Technology in Education in Washington, DC, says, "The library media specialist is at once a teacher, an instructional partner, an information specialist, and a program administrator. They collaborate with teachers, administrators, and others to prepare students for future success." Being adaptable, resourceful, and creative makes it easier for library media specialists to successfully fill all these roles.

On the Job

Employers

Library media specialists work in elementary and secondary schools. With specialized training, they may also work in colleges and universities as academic librarians, in public libraries, in law offices as law librarians, and for private corporations as specialist librarians.

Working Conditions

Most school library media centers are pleasant, busy places. The noise level is usually low to moderate. Library media specialists generally have a private office located in the media center. Their work schedule is usually the same as that of teachers. Typically, they work approximately 185 to 190 days per year. This translates to about ten months per year, with a two-month break in the summer. Those who work in schools on a nontraditional year-round schedule typically work forty-five days in a row with fifteen days off, or sixty days with twenty days off. Work hours are set by the local school district. A typical school day starts at 8:00 a.m. and ends at 3:00 p.m. Some library media specialists stay after hours to confer with teachers or sponsor student book clubs.

While performing the duties of this job, these educators walk, stand, stoop, kneel, crouch, and reach a lot. They often have to lift and move books, computers, audiovisual equipment, and furniture in the library, which can lead to back injuries.

Earnings

According to the BLS, annual salaries for most library media specialists range from about $33,380 to $86,320. Mean annual salaries are reported to be about $59,560. Pay depends on the location of the job and the individual's level of education, length of service, and training. Most library media specialists receive employee benefits that include health insurance, paid sick and vacation days, and retirement benefits. In addition, the federal government will cancel up to 100 percent of federal Perkins student loans for librarians who work for one school year in a school that serves low-income students. Partial loan cancellation is also possible through the federal Public Service Loan Forgiveness program.

Opportunities for Advancement

In most school districts, librarians are paid on the basis of their years of service, education level, and performance evaluation. Individuals with good performance evaluations, advanced training and education, and many years of service are paid at the top of the pay scale. In media centers with more than one librarian, which is common in large high schools, library media specialists can advance to a supervisory position. School librarians who take advanced course work and earn a school administrator credential can advance to district library director, a position that entails overseeing all the librarians and library services in a school district. They can also hold positions as curriculum specialists, principals, assistant principals, and district-level administrators. By taking graduate courses specific to a particular specialty field, these professionals can qualify to work in academic libraries, public libraries, or law or medical libraries. Possessing a doctorate qualifies individuals to advance to faculty positions in college and university library science and instructional technology programs, giving them the opportunity to teach the next generation of library media specialists.

What Is the Future Outlook for Library Media Specialists?

The BLS estimates that employment for librarians will grow by 7 percent from 2012 to 2022, which is less than average. However, according to the American Library Association, more than three in five librarians will become eligible for retirement in the next ten years. Personnel will be needed to replace these professionals. Also, approximately 25 percent of school libraries do not currently have a certified library media specialist on staff. Filling these positions with qualified individuals is a top priority. Moreover, as of 2014 there is a shortage of library media specialists in certain areas of the United States, such as Arkansas and western Tennessee, as well as in inner cities and rural areas.

Find Out More

American Association of School Librarians (AASL)
50 E. Huron St.
Chicago, IL 60611
phone: (312) 280-4382
e mail: aasl@ala.org
website: www.aasl.org

The AASL is a professional organization of school library media specialists and a division of the American Library Association. It provides a wealth of information about a career as a school librarian.

American Library Association (ALA)
50 E. Huron St.
Chicago, IL 60611
phone: (800) 545-2433
e-mail: ala@ala.org
website: www.ala.org

The ALA is the largest library association in the world. It provides information about issues concerning libraries and librarians, including information about scholarships and ALA-accredited degree programs.

American Society for Information Science and Technology (ASIS)
1320 Fenwick Ln., Suite 510
Silver Spring, MD 20910
phone: (301) 495-0810
website: www.asis.org

The ASIS is a professional organization of information specialists working in various careers, including librarian. It offers information about accredited library and information science programs and a job list.

Teacher Certification Degrees
website: www.teachercertificationdegrees.com

This website provides information on various careers in education. Its school librarian page provides data on education and certification requirements and on employment, as well as profiles of school librarians.

School Counselor

What Does a School Counselor Do?

School counselors work in elementary, secondary, and postsecondary schools. They are leaders, instructors, student advocates, facilitators, and mental health professionals. Although their jobs differ depending on the age group they serve, their primary role is to support the academic, emotional, and social development of students. They do this through prevention programs and by addressing existing problems. Because students' needs differ with age, a counselor's primary focus depends on the student population. For example, postsecondary counselors focus on student wellness. Their main role is helping students cope with emotional and personal issues that affect their well-being and academic performance. High school counselors concentrate on helping students explore career options and postsecondary training. They advise students on college and technical school choices, assist with admission applications and financial aid forms, and write reference letters to college admission officers or possible employers. They also spend a lot of time arranging students' class schedules. Middle school counselors concentrate on helping students

At a Glance:
School Counselor

Minimum Educational Requirements
Master's degree

Personal Qualities
Nonjudgmental
Trustworthy

Certification and Licensing
School counselor certification
National certification

Working Conditions
Indoors in elementary, secondary, and postsecondary schools

Salary Range
From about $31,850 to $86,870

Number of Jobs
As of 2014 about 262,300

Future Job Outlook
Better than average

make the transition from elementary to secondary school. This often involves providing classroom instruction in goal setting and study skills. Elementary school counselors deal more with behavioral and social issues.

Elementary and secondary school counselors play other roles, too. They are involved in organizing, coordinating, and scheduling standardized tests and analyzing test data. They coordinate special programs, including peer mediation programs, that empower students and improve their ability to make good decisions. Peer mediation programs provide counselors to train and oversee students as they help their peers resolve misunderstandings. Counselors also provide classroom instruction on topics like bullying and coping with peer pressure. And they help new students acclimate to the school. For example, in order to make new students feel welcome and special, Mindy Willard, the American School Counselor Association's Counselor of the Year for 2013, hosts a quarterly Breakfast with the Counselor for new students. As she and the students breakfast together, she answers questions about the school and surveys how her guests' transition is going. If she finds a student is having trouble adjusting, she schedules a counseling session for that youngster.

College counselors work mainly with individuals, couples, and small groups whom they see via scheduled appointments. Attending college is a major transition for students. It is the first time many young people are on their own. Some have trouble handling their newfound independence and the stress of college life. It is not uncommon for college students to develop emotional issues that impact their academic performance. Through counseling sessions, postsecondary counselors help individuals cope with their problems.

Elementary and secondary school counselors work with individuals and small groups, too. They may counsel small groups of students with behavioral issues or hold impromptu counseling sessions with individual students who are extremely upset or acting out. And they confer with parents, teachers, administrators, school social workers, school nurses, and school psychologists in an effort to meet each student's needs. When students' problems go beyond the range of counselors to deal with, they refer students to social and health agencies that can help them.

Keeping up with paperwork is another part of all counselors' job. No matter the age level they work with, school counselors must keep accurate records of counseling sessions, clients' progress, and outside referrals.

Clearly, counselors wear many different "hats" and have a lot of variety in their day, As Raleigh, North Carolina, elementary school counselor Rebecca Atkins explains in an interview on Teaching.org, "I really like the diversity of duties. My personality is such that I would not like to be in one classroom all day or sitting at a desk all day. Being a school counselor means that every day is different and brings new challenges."

How Do You Become a School or College Counselor?

Education

To prepare for a career as a counselor, in high school students should take classes that ready them for college, including classes in psychology, which give them insight into the workings of the human mind. Educational requirements for this career vary by state, school district, and school. The basic requirement is a bachelor's degree plus approximately thirty hours of specified courses at the graduate level. However, most states and schools require a master's degree in counseling. This entails four years beyond high school earning a bachelor's degree, followed by one to two years earning a master's degree. Some states require elementary and secondary school counselors to have a teacher's license and previous teaching experience.

Graduate course work typically includes instruction in human growth and development, individual and group counseling, and grief counseling. Depending on the state, course work may include field experience in the form of a supervised practicum and/or a supervised internship.

Certification and Licensing

Certification and licensing requirements vary by state and school. Most public schools require elementary and secondary counselors to hold a valid teacher's certificate and a school counselor credential. Most postsecondary schools require that counselors hold national certification. In both cases individuals must successfully complete specified graduate-level course work from an accredited counseling program. Applicants for national certification must also successfully complete about three hundred hours of supervised field experience.

Depending on the state, applicants for a school counselor credential may be required to have previous teaching experience and pass a comprehensive school counselor exam. In most cases a school counselor credential permits counselors to work with students from prekindergarten through high school. Applicants for national certification must successfully complete the National Counselor Examination administered by the National Board for Certified Counselors.

Volunteer Work and Internships

Volunteer work and internships are a good way to learn about and gain experience in school counseling. Serving as an intern or volunteering as a tutor in a school, community center, or a youth service organization like Big Brothers Big Sisters gives individuals the opportunity to interact with children and young adults and see if they enjoy working with young people. It also provides prospective counselors with experience in explaining concepts and helps them develop patience, two skills that counselors need. Most universities help students find volunteer and internship positions, and most organizations seeking counseling volunteers and interns provide practical training.

Other activities, too, can help young people gain experience that may help them be effective counselors. For instance, becoming a member of a dorm leadership team, especially as a hall advisor or peer mentor, gives individuals an opportunity to counsel incoming students and peers.

Skills and Personality

Counselors should genuinely care about others. They should be able to relate well and be sensitive to people of diverse cultural backgrounds. Being compassionate and nonjudgmental goes a long way in this job. Sometimes the young people school counselors work with are angry or hostile. They often take out their frustrations on the counselor. Counselors must be able to disregard any negative emotions they may have toward a student and focus on treating all students equally. They also should be trustworthy and ethical. In order for students to open up, they must trust the counselor and feel assured that nothing they say in a session will ever be divulged unless mandated by law.

Being a good listener and speaker is essential. During a counseling session, counselors must focus their attention on the young people they are counseling, listen carefully to what they are saying without interrupting, and ask appropriate questions. Good communication skills are also vital for instructing classes and conferring with parents, administrators, faculty, and staff. Indeed, a large part of this career involves communicating with others and making connections. Therefore, being able to work as part of a team is vital.

Another key personality trait for this profession is flexibility. Even though school counselors plan for each day, crises arise, and counselors must be flexible enough to change their schedule and deal with events as they unfold. Plus they should be able to handle stress well. Dealing with serious issues is part of the job. School counselors must be able to set boundaries and distance themselves emotionally from their students' problems in order to do their job effectively.

On the Job

Employers

School counselors work in public and private schools and in colleges and universities. They also are employed by private international schools throughout the world.

Working Conditions

School counselors usually have their own office so they can hear student's problems while maintaining an atmosphere of privacy. Elementary school counselors usually work approximately 185 to 190 days per year. This translates to about ten months per year, with a two-month break in the summer. Some middle and high school counselors work part of the summer arranging student class schedules. Post-secondary counselors usually work year-round. Work hours vary. A typical school day for elementary and secondary counselors usually starts at 8:00 a.m. and ends at 3:00 p.m. College counselors usually work a forty-hour week.

Most counselors have a heavy caseload. As of 2014 the average ratio of students to school counselors in the United States was 471 to 1. The national recommendation for the ratio of students to school counselors is 200 to 1. Handling so many students can be frustrating and stressful.

Earnings

The BLS reports that salaries for most counselors range from about $31,850 to $86,870. The pay depends on the location of the job and the individual's level of education, length of service, and training. The BLS reports a mean annual salary of $53,610 for school counselors. Most school counselors receive employee benefits that include health insurance, paid sick and vacation days, and retirement benefits. In addition, under the Public Service Loan Forgiveness program, some elementary and secondary school counselors may qualify for partial forgiveness of student loans. To qualify, counselors must be employed by a public school and have made 120 payments on qualified loans before the remaining balance of the loan is forgiven.

Opportunities for Advancement

In most school districts and colleges, counselors are paid on the basis of their years of service, education level, and performance evaluation. Individuals with good performance evaluations, advanced training and education, and many years of service are paid at the top of the pay scale. These individuals are most likely to advance to counseling directors, professionals who supervise all the counselors in a school district. With additional graduate-level course work in school ad-ministration and licensure, elementary and secondary counselors can become school principals, assistant principals, and district-level ad-ministrators. Additional course work in specialized counseling fields qualifies school counselors to become career counselors in colleges and universities or go into private practice. Counselors with a doctoral degree can advance to faculty positions in college and university counseling education programs.

What Is the Future Outlook for School Counselors?

The BLS estimates that employment for counselors will grow by 12 percent between 2012 and 2022. This figure is slightly higher than all occupations. However, in an effort to decrease violence in schools, the federal government has called for more counselors in schools. This initiative could further increase job growth in this field.

Find Out More

American Counseling Association
5999 Stevenson Ave.
Alexandria, VA 22304-3304
phone: (800) 347-6647
website: www.counseling.org

This organization offers information about different counseling careers, certification and licensing, and graduate school counseling programs.

American School Counselor Association (ASCA)
1101 King St., Suite 625
Alexandria, VA 22314-2957
phone: (800) 306-4722
e-mail: asca@schoolcounselor.org
website: www.schoolcounselor.org

The ASCA provides information on many aspects of school counseling, including information about certification and licensing, the role of a school counselor, and college loan forgiveness.

Education Portal
website: http://education-portal.com

This website provides information on various careers in education. It contains a school counselor article that describes the job and educational requirements, as well as a school counselor career video.

National Board for Certified Counselors (NBCC)
3 Terrace Way
Greensboro, NC 27403
phone: (336) 547-0607
e-mail: nbcc@nbcc.org
website: www.nbcc.org

The NBCC administers the National Counselor's Exam. Its website provides information about national certification.

Special Education Teacher

What Does a Special Education Teacher Do?

Special education teachers instruct students with physical, mental, and emotional disabilities. These include specific learning disorders, mental retardation, and brain injuries, as well as visual, speech, hearing, and orthopedic impairments. Students may also have emotional, social, or behavioral disorders. It is up to special education teachers to personalize and adapt instruction to suit each student's unique learning challenges. To facilitate this, in collaboration with other education professionals and parents, special educators create an individualized education plan (IEP), which identifies specific learning goals for each student. Special educators plan their lessons based on each student's IEP and administer assessments throughout the school year to measure each student's progress.

In any given day special educators can be found providing instruction to small groups of students. Lessons are custom-

At a Glance:
Special Education Teacher

Minimum Educational Requirements
Bachelor's degree

Personal Qualities
Patient
Even-tempered

Certification and Licensing
Teacher's license with a special education credential

Working Conditions
Indoors in schools

Salary Range
About $33,770 to $82,000

Number of Jobs
As of 2014 about 473,000

Future Job Outlook
Below average

ized to suit each pupil's particular abilities, needs, and learning style. Instructional strategies may involve teachers breaking down a task into many small steps or turning lessons into games. They may use physical activities, songs, raps, or rhymes to reinforce concepts, or they may employ adaptive learning equipment like braille readers or communication software to facilitate learning.

Some special education students attend regular education classrooms in a method known as inclusion or mainstreaming. To help these students succeed, special education teachers collaborate with regular education teachers. Guided by the special educator's expertise, the two prepare lesson plans and go over learning strategies and adaptive techniques that meet the students' unique learning challenges. When students need special accommodations, such as extra time to complete an assignment or a test, special education teachers make sure appropriate accommodations are provided.

In addition to dealing with academic concerns, special educators help learners develop life skills. This may involve working on strategies designed to improve social skills or to better cope with anger or behavioral issues. Or it may involve teaching severely disabled pupils self-care skills. In an effort to prepare learners for employment, some special educators provide high school students with vocational training in fields like hospitality trades, construction, and child care. Some special educators go beyond preparing students for a career; they help students gain employment. For example, in her twenty-five-year career as a New Mexico special educator, Nita Tabet linked up her graduating students with local employers. "I'd go out and talk to business owners in person," she says. "If they agreed to interview one of my students, I helped the students prepare for their interviews by instructing them in how to dress, what to say, how to act." Over the years, she has helped dozens of students gain long-term employment.

In addition to working with students, special education teachers are responsible for all the paperwork that regular education teachers are responsible for, as well as paperwork specific to special education. These educators also spend a lot of time interacting with social agencies and other education professionals. In addition, most special educators have a teacher's aide assigned to them. Supervising the paraprofessional is another part of a special education teacher's job.

How Do You Become a Special Education Teacher?

Education

To prepare for a career as a special education teacher, high school students should take classes that ready them for college. If a prospective special educator plans to work in an area in which many people do not speak English, studying a foreign language, especially Spanish, is helpful, as is learning American Sign Language.

Special education teachers must have a minimum of a bachelor's degree from an accredited teacher education program. Most candidates major in special education. Course work includes required liberal arts and science classes and professional education courses. The latter includes classes that prepare candidates to work with students with learning challenges. Students interested in working with a particular age group—such as preschool children or a specific special education specialty such as the severely handicapped—focus their course work in these areas. Supervised field experience and a semester of student teaching are other essential parts of the program. Individuals with a bachelor's degree who have not attended a teacher education program can qualify for a position as a special educator by earning a master's degree in special education.

Certification and Licensing

All fifty states and the District of Columbia require special education teachers to be licensed. Licensing requirements vary by state. Many states practice license reciprocity, allowing educators to transfer their license between states. In some states special education teachers receive a general education license to teach kindergarten through grade twelve and an additional credential in special education. Depending on the state, this credential may cover a variety of disability categories, or it may be for a specific specialty area such as learning disabilities or emotional and behavioral disorders. Licensing requirements for employment in private schools vary.

To become licensed and certified, prospective special education teachers must earn a bachelor's degree from an accredited education program, successfully complete student teaching, pass a written basic skills exam, and pass an exam specific to special education. Some states allow teachers licensed in other fields to earn a special education credential by successfully completing the special education content-specific exam. Some states allow unlicensed individuals with a bachelor's degree to teach special education while completing an accelerated education program under an alternative certification program.

Volunteer Work and Internships

Individuals interested in a career as a special education teacher can experience what it is like to work with people with disabilities by volunteering in a school, day care facility, residential facility, hospital, or community program that serves people with special needs. Working as a camp counselor in a summer camp for children with special needs, volunteering at a local Special Olympics, or tutoring a special education student are other options. Participating in an internship program is also a useful means of learning more about the profession, and many colleges help match students with internship programs. In addition, organizations like the Children's Defense Fund recruit college students to serve as interns in summer programs that involve working with children of varying backgrounds and needs. Job shadowing a special education teacher is another good way to learn about the profession.

Skills and Personality

Individuals who like helping others and are patient, emotionally stable, and even-tempered are good candidates for special educators. Being in a special education classroom can be frustrating for both teachers and students. Special education students often take longer to master a concept than other students, and it is not uncommon for them to forget concepts that they have already learned. Special educators have to use a wide variety of teaching methods to encourage, motivate, and instruct reluctant and frustrated students. Creativity and flexibility are essential, as are patience, compassion, and acceptance of differences in others. At the same time, these professionals need to be calm and firm. They must maintain self-control even when students are angry or agitated. And because students often take out their frustrations on their teacher, special educators need to have thick skins. They cannot take such outpourings personally. It also helps if these professionals are upbeat in nature and have a sense of humor.

Since special educators interact with many people every day, being cooperative and having good oral and written communication skills are also essential.

On the Job

Employers

According to the BLS, most special education teachers work in public and private schools. They are also employed by state education agencies, residential facilities, hospitals, child care centers, and social agencies. Some are self-employed tutors or work for a tutoring company.

Working Conditions

Most special educators work in schools. Some teach in self-contained classrooms in which they instruct the same group of students in multiple subjects all day long. Others instruct rotating groups of students in specific subjects for a set time each day. Some team teach with regular educators. Some work with homebound students or with infants and toddlers in the children's homes. These educators provide their own transportation.

Most work approximately 185 to 190 days per year. Traditionally, this translates to ten months per year, with a two-month break in the summer. Those who work in schools on a nontraditional year-round schedule typically work forty-five days in a row with fifteen days off, or sixty days with twenty days off. Then the cycle begins again. Work hours are set by the local school district. Special educators work standard teacher hours. A typical school day starts at 8:00 a.m. and ends at 3:00 p.m. However, special education teachers may meet with parents before or after school and often grade papers, write lesson plans, or complete other paperwork at home.

Earnings

The BLS reports that salaries for special education teachers range from about $33,770 to $82,000. Pay depends on the location of the job and the educator's level of education, length of service, and training. The BLS reports a mean annual salary of $60,410 for secondary school special education teachers and $56,690 for elementary school special education teachers. Since salaries for secondary and elementary educators follow the same scale in most school districts, the difference in mean salary may be due to the fact that secondary teachers are more likely than elementary teachers to serve as a department head or a coach, for which they receive extra pay. According to the BLS, mean wages for secondary special educators/elementary special educators are highest in the following states: New York, $75,470/$70,010; Rhode Island, $73,870/$72,380; and Connecticut, $71,810/$71,590. Most special education teachers receive employee benefits that include health insurance, paid sick and vacation days, and retirement benefits. In addition, the federal government offers college loan forgiveness and cancellation programs for special education teachers. Up to 100 percent of federal Perkins loans can be canceled for individuals who serve as special education teachers for one full school year. Federal teacher loan forgiveness of up to $17,500 is available for other types of student loans for special education teachers who work in the field for five consecutive school years. In addition, educators who teach in a state-identified subject shortage area, which usually includes special education, may qualify for loan forgiveness through their state or city.

Opportunities for Advancement

In most school districts teachers are paid on the basis of their years of service, education level, and performance evaluation. Special education teachers with good performance evaluations, a master's degree or higher, and twenty or more years of service are paid at the top of the pay scale. Possessing experience and a master's degree can advance special educators to positions as department heads, program directors, educational diagnosticians, or curriculum specialists. A master's degree in school administration qualifies special education teachers to become school principals, assistant principals, private school directors, and district-level administrators. Possessing a doctorate qualifies individuals to advance to faculty positions in college and university special education programs. Some special educators own and operate tutoring or testing services.

What Is the Future Outlook for Special Education Teachers?

The BLS estimates that the number of special education teaching positions in kindergarten through secondary school will increase by about 6 percent through 2020, which is slower than average. However, there is a chronic shortage of qualified special education teachers in school districts throughout the United States, with the greatest shortages in inner cities, low-income schools, and rural areas. For the 2014–2015 school year, the Department of Education reported critical shortages of special education teachers in forty-eight states and the District of Columbia. This is an ongoing problem. Similar shortages have been reported for the past decade. As a result, many special education positions are being filled by educators teaching out of their field of expertise or by unlicensed substitute teachers. Filling these positions with qualified special educators is a top priority. Moreover, job openings continuously arise to replace special educators who leave the field. Teaching special education can be stressful, and approximately one in ten special education teachers resign after one year.

Find Out More

Council for Exceptional Children (CEC)
2900 Crystal Dr., Suite 1000
Arlington, VA 22202-3557
phone: (888) 232-7733
e-mail: service@cec.sped.org
website: www.cec.sped.org

The CEC provides information on a wide range of special education topics, including resources for educators, a special education teacher's blog, special education job profiles, and a job board.

Learning Disabilities Association of America
4156 Library Rd.
Pittsburgh, PA 15234-1349
phone: (412) 341-1515
e-mail: info@ldaamerica.org
website: http://ldaamerica.org

This organization's goal is to empower people with learning disabilities. It provides information about various learning disabilities and special education, including journals, publications, and videos.

National Association of Special Education Teachers (NASET)
1250 Connecticut Ave. NW, Suite 200
Washington, DC 20036-2643
phone: (800) 754-4421
e-mail: contactus@naset.org
website: www.naset.org

The NASET is a professional organization of special education teachers and students preparing to be special educators. It provides information about the career, professional journals, and job lists.

US Department of Education
Office of Special Education and Rehabilitative Services (OSERS)
400 Maryland Ave. SW
Washington, DC 20202-7100
phone: (202) 254-7468
website: www2.ed.gov/about/offices/list/osers/osep

The OSERS provides information about special education programs, student loans, and student loan forgiveness programs.

Interview with a Special Education Teacher

Steve Speegle is an eighth-grade special education teacher at Gadsden Middle School in Anthony, New Mexico. He has worked in education for twenty-seven years. He started his career as a special education teacher, served as a school administrator, then returned to teaching special education. He spoke with the author about his career.

Q: Why did you become a special education teacher?

A: I did not plan on it. I needed a job and they needed special ed. teachers. I got into an alternative certification program. They gave me a year to get certified. I took two graduate level courses, challenged the licensing exam and passed it, and was allowed to teach. Then I took more classes. I didn't really know what I was getting into with special ed., but once I got into it, I didn't want to teach anything else. I really liked it, and I still feel that way.

Q: Can you describe a typical day?

A: I get to work about 7:15. One reason I arrive early is to make sure I have access to the copier. There are only two machines for all the teachers to use. But a lot of what I do is without copies. A lot of my kids are visual learners, so I google images and prepare them for use in lessons. I also go early to plan and to prepare, and to do IEPs [individualized education plans]. It takes me about two hours to fill in all the information. I have a case load of thirteen special ed. students. I have to conduct and chair five IEP meetings a month, and that's above and beyond all my teaching duties, and it is federally mandated. I also attend meetings about special ed. policies and changes before school.

At 8:30, class starts. The first thing I have is ICAT—Individualized Career Advisement Team. Federal law mandates that special ed. programs help students transition to the real world. In this class, students talk about careers and set career goals. I correlate IEP education goals with the student's career goals.

From 9 to 10:30, I have an academic skills class. These are lower functioning kiddos that need extra help in language arts. I try to do as much of the 8th grade curriculum with them as possible, but at their reading level, which might be a third grade level.

From 10:30 to 12, I have a resource class, which [is for] higher functioning kids. I get them ready for inclusion [attending regular education classes]. I teach them the same thing a regular 8th grade language arts teacher does, but slowly and in more steps. For example, tomorrow we're doing a directed reading activity about a novel, and they'll write a book report on it. We'll read the book in class together first, which will take a few weeks. Then, we'll do an outline for the book report together. Then we'll do research on the Internet about the author and the setting. Then they'll write their book reports in class on the computers I have in my classroom, and print them out.

I have a thirty-minute lunch, followed by a 1½ hour [preparation] period. That's when we have Professional Learning Communities; that is, special education department conferences with administrators to go over test scores, discuss schedules, instruction strategies, and disseminate data. We do this three days a week. The other days, I actually plan.

At 2:15 I teach another academic skills class just like in the morning. I go home at 3:45.

Q: What do you like most and least about your job?
A: Most, I love the kids. I like being in school with them. When all the other stuff like meetings and paper work bug me, I can just close my door and teach.

Least, the meetings and the paper work. They really bury us with paper work. Special ed. teachers have to do all the regular ed. paperwork and the special ed. paperwork.

Q: What personal qualities do you find most valuable to this type of work?

A: Empathy, the ability to listen, to be non-judgmental, the ability to reach in and grab a kid by the heart. I don't care how ornery a kid is, I let them know I want to help them and prepare them for high school. You have to make it fun to learn, and give them a comfortable, supportive environment. You have to be trustworthy. These kids bring a lot of problems with them from home. They need to feel they can trust you and confide in you.

Q: What advice do you have for students who might be interested in this career?

A: It's very rewarding, but you aren't going to get rich.

Other Careers in Education

Academic librarian
Adult literacy and high
  school equivalency diploma
  instructor
Archivist
Bilingual teacher
Career and technical education
  teachers
Career counselor
Coach
Dance instructor
Educational software developer
Employee training specialist
Health educator
Library technician

Museum teacher
Preschool director
Public librarian
Registrar
School bus driver
School custodian
School nurse
School psychologist
School secretary
School social worker
Speech language pathologist
Substitute teacher
Teacher's aide
Textbook editor

Editor's note: The online *Occupational Outlook Handbook* of the US Department of Labor's Bureau of Labor Statistics is an excellent source of information on jobs in hundreds of career fields, including many of those listed here. The *Occupational Outlook Handbook* may be accessed online at www.bls.gov/ooh.

Index

Note: Boldface page numbers indicate illustrations.

American Association of School
    Librarians (AASL), 57
American Association of School
    Superintendents (AASA), 40
American Association of University
    Administrators (AAUA), 41
American Association of University
    Professors (AAUP), 14, 15
American Counseling Association, 64
American Federation of Teachers (AFT),
    48–49
    Higher Education Division, 15–16
American Library Association (ALA),
    53, 56, 57
American School Counselor Association
    (ASCA), 64
American Society for Information
    Science and Technology (ASIS), 57
assistant principals, 35
Association for Supervision and
    Curriculum Development (ASCD), 23

Big Brothers Big Sisters, 61
Big Future by the College Board
    (website), 23
Bureau of Labor Statistics (BLS)
    on college professor, 15
    on curriculum developer, 21–22, 23
    on early childhood educator, 30, 31, 32
    on education administrator, 39, 40
    on K–12 teacher, 46, 48
    on library media specialist, 55, 56
    on school counselor, 63, 64
    on special education teacher, 70, 71, 72
    on total US employment/growth in
        educational employment, 7
Busby, John, 52

Child Development Associate (CDA)
    Credential, 28–29
Children's Defense Fund, 69
college presidents, 35, 39
college professors
    advancement opportunities, 14–15
    certification/licensing, 9, 11–12
    education, 9, 11
    employers of, 13
    future outlook for, 9, 15
    information resources on, 15–16
    number of jobs, 9
    roles of, 9–11
    salaries/earnings, 9, 14
    skills/personality traits, 9, 12–13
    volunteer work/internships, 12
    working conditions, 9, 13
Council for Exceptional Children
    (CEC), 72
Council for Professional Recognition, 32
curriculum developers
    advancement opportunities, 22
    certification/licensing, 17, 20
    education, 17, 19
    employers of, 21–22
    future outlook for, 17, 23
    information resources on, 23–24
    number of jobs, 17
    roles of, 17–19
    salaries/earnings, 17, 22
    skills/personality traits, 17, 21
    volunteer work/internships, 20–21
    working conditions, 17, 22

Department of Education, US, 47, 72, 73
district administrators, 35

early childhood educators
    advancement opportunities, 31–32
    certification/licensing, 25, 28–29

education, 25, 27–28
employers of, 30
future outlook, 25, 32
information resources on, 32–33
number of jobs, 25
roles of, 25–27
salaries/earnings, 25, 31
skills/personality traits, 25, 29–30
volunteer work/internships, 29
working conditions, 25, 30–31
earnings. *See* salaries/earnings
education administrators
    advancement opportunities, 39–40
    certification/licensing, 34, 37
    education, 34, 36
    employers of, 38
    future outlook, 34, 40
    information resources on, 40–41
    number of jobs, 34
    roles of, 34–36
    salaries/earnings, 34, 39
    skills/personality traits, 34, 37–38
    volunteer work/internships, 37
    working conditions, 34, 38–39
educational careers
    growth of employment in, 7
    salary ranges/ratings of, 6
Education Careers Review (website), 23
education/educational requirements
    for college professors, 9, 11
    for curriculum developers, 17, 19
    for early childhood educators, 25,
        27–28
    for education administrators, 34, 36
    for K–12 teachers, 42, 43–44
    for library media specialists, 50, 52–53
    for school counselors, 58, 60
    for special education teachers, 66, 68
Education Portal (website), 24, 32, 64–65
English as a second language (ESL/
    ESOL) instructors, 5

Favre, Megan, 43
Future Educators Association (FEA), 49

Greene, John Robert, 10–11
Griffith, Michael, 10

Head Start teachers, 28
Herbst, Susan, 9
Huesken, Gerald, 35

individualized education plans (IEPs), 66
information resources
    for college professor, 15–16
    for curriculum developers, 23–24
    for early childhood educator, 32–33
    for education administrator, 40–41
    for K–12 teacher, 48–49
    on library media specialist, 57
    on school counselor, 64–65
    on special education teacher, 72–73

Knezek, Don, 54
Kornfeld, Amos, 35
K–12 teachers
    advancement opportunities, 48
    certification/licensing, 42, 44
    education, 42, 43–44
    employers of, 46
    future outlook, 42, 48
    information resources on, 48–49
    number of jobs, 42
    roles of, 42–43
    salaries/earnings, 42, 46–48
    skills/personality traits, 42, 45
    volunteer work/internships, 44–45
    working conditions, 42, 46

Learning Disabilities Association of
    America, 73
library media specialists
    advancement opportunities, 56
    certification/licensing, 50, 53
    education, 50, 52–53
    employers of, 55
    future outlook, 50, 56–57
    information resources on, 57
    number of jobs, 50
    roles of, 50–52
    salaries/earnings, 50, 55–56
    skills/personality traits, 50, 54–55
    volunteer work/internships, 53–54
    working conditions, 50, 55

National Association for the Education

of Young Children (NAEYC), 32–33
National Association of Elementary
    School Principals, 41
National Association of Scholars (NAS),
    16
National Association of Secondary
    School Principals (NASSP), 41
National Association of Special
    Education Teachers (NASET), 73
National Board for Certified Counselors
    (NBCC), 65
National Education Association (NEA),
    49
    Higher Education Division, 16
Nodolski, Trish, 26

Perkins student loans, 47, 56, 71
PreSchool Education.com (website), 33
preschool teachers. *See* early childhood
    educators
Public Service Loan Forgiveness
    program, 56, 63

Rycik, Mary, 7–8

salaries/earnings
    for college professors, 9, 14
    for curriculum developers, 17, 22
    for early childhood educators, 25, 31
    for education administrators, 34, 39
    for educational positions, 6
    for K–12 teachers, 42, 46–48
    for library media specialists, 50, 55–56
    for school counselors, 58, 63
    for special education teachers, 66, 71
school counselors
    advancement opportunities, 63–64
    certification/licensing, 58, 60–61

education, 58, 60
employers of, 62
future outlook, 58, 64
information resources on, 64–65
number of jobs, 58
roles of, 58–60
salaries/earnings, 58, 63
skills/personality traits, 58, 61–62
volunteer work/internships, 61
working conditions, 58, 62–63
school superintendents, 35
special education teachers
    advancement opportunities, 71–72
    certification/licensing, 66, 68–69
    education, 66, 68
    employers of, 70
    future outlook, 66, 72
    information resources on, 72–73
    interview with, 74–76
    number of jobs, 66
    roles of, 66–67
    salaries/earnings, 66, 71
    skills/personality traits, 66, 69–70
    volunteer work/internships, 69
    working conditions, 66, 70
Speegle, Steve, 74–76
students, numbers in US elementary/
    secondary schools, 4

Tabet, Nita, 67
Teach California (website), 49
Teacher Certification Degrees (website),
    57
teachers. *See* K–12 teachers
tenure, of college professors, 13, 14–15

Willard, Mindy, 59